PRESIDENTIAL PERSPECTIVES

THE NEW NATION
THROUGH THE EYES OF
GEORGE WASHINGTON

by Anita Yasuda

Content Consultant
Richard Dougherty, PhD
Professor, Politics Department
University of Dallas

Core Library

An Imprint of Abdo Publishing
abdopublishing.com

abdopublishing.com

Published by Abdo Publishing, a division of ABDO, PO Box 398166, Minneapolis, Minnesota 55439. Copyright © 2016 by Abdo Consulting Group, Inc. International copyrights reserved in all countries. No part of this book may be reproduced in any form without written permission from the publisher. Core Library™ is a trademark and logo of Abdo Publishing.

Printed in the United States of America, North Mankato, Minnesota
082015
012016

THIS BOOK CONTAINS
RECYCLED MATERIALS

Cover Photo: Library of Congress
Interior Photos: Library of Congress, 1; North Wind Picture Archives, 4, 22, 30, 32, 34; Currier & Ives/Library of Congress, 6, 45; John Trumbull, 8, 24; Red Line Editorial, 11, 16; Pendleton's Lithography/Library of Congress, 14; Bettmann/Corbis, 18, 27; Metropolitan Museum of Art, 37; Stock Montage/Getty Images, 38; Stefano Bianchetti/Corbis, 40

Editor: Jon Westmark
Series Designer: Laura Polzin

Library of Congress Control Number: 2015945409

Cataloging-in-Publication Data
Yasuda, Anita.
 The New Nation through the eyes of George Washington / Anita Yasuda.
   p. cm. -- (Presidential perspectives)
ISBN 978-1-68078-033-8 (lib. bdg.)
Includes bibliographical references and index.
1. United States--History--Revolution, 1775-1783--Juvenile literature. 2. Washington, George, 1732-1799--Juvenile literature. 3. Presidents--United States--Juvenile literature.   I. Title.
973.4--dc23

                                                                    2015945409

CONTENTS

THE RELUCTANT PRESIDENT

The crowd cheered loudly as George Washington stepped onto the balcony of Federal Hall in New York City on April 30, 1789. People had started arriving early in the morning. The crowd now filled the square. Some people even sat on rooftops for the important occasion. Everyone wanted to see His Excellency take the oath of office to become the first president of the United States.

George Washington took the oath of office to become US president on April 30, 1789.

Washington became a legend as general of the Continental Army during the Revolutionary War.

During the ceremony, Washington swore to "preserve, protect, and defend the Constitution of the United States." The air hummed with excitement. Celebrations filled every corner of the city. But Washington was not filled with joy. The former leader of the Continental Army was uneasy.

Washington later described his feelings in his diary. He said the presidency was unlike any job he held before. Washington questioned if he had the skills to lead the country. The American people believed he did. All the states' representatives had voted for him.

The General's Commission

In the 1600s, Britain started 13 colonies on the eastern coast of North America. By the 1770s, many colonists were unhappy with British rule. They were upset they did not have representation in Britain. The war for the colonies' independence, the Revolutionary War (1775–1783), broke out in 1775. Washington became a legend during the war. He was the leader of the army that fought against British rule. After many battles, the newly formed United States of America achieved victory over the British.

When the war was over, many thought Washington was the clear choice to lead the country. But in December 1783, he did something

Washington stepped down as leader of the Continental Army on December 23, 1783.

surprising. Washington stepped down as leader of the Continental army. He believed the new nation needed elected representatives.

Washington retired to his home, Mount Vernon, in Virginia. But his time away from public life did not last long. He soon realized the 13 states were not acting like one nation. A set of laws known as the Articles of Confederation held the states together. Washington thought the articles were too weak. State governments held more power than the national government.

Washington's concerns about the Articles of Confederation were realized in 1786. Daniel Shays, a former US army officer, started a rebellion in Massachusetts. Shays and other Massachusetts farmers were angry with the state government. They felt it was not doing all it could to help them with their debts. But the US government could do little to fight the rebellion. Congress did not have the money for an army. Under the Articles of Confederation, only states could collect taxes. The Massachusetts governor established a militia that quickly put down the rebellion.

Constitutional Convention

Washington believed the rebellion proved the country was in need of change. He urged state leaders to create a stronger national government. Twelve states sent delegates to Philadelphia, Pennsylvania, to represent them in talks about the national

Articles of Confederation

The Articles of Confederation contained a set of laws to govern the United States. Some of the delegates who drafted the laws did not want the country to have a strong central government. They feared it would create a nation that was no freer than the one they had under British rule. The articles did not create an executive branch, so there was no president. There was no judiciary, or federal court. But there was a legislative branch. The articles limited the legislature's ability to control trade and taxes. And it did not have the power to enforce laws.

government. Washington was not going to attend the convention. He called the job of reforming the articles a "sea of troubles." But his friends encouraged him to go. They felt without him the conference might not succeed.

Washington reluctantly went. But he did not take part in the debates. He led the convention. When arguments became too heated, he kept the delegates on track. Four months later, the United States had a

	George Washington	John Adams	Samuel Huntington	John Jay	John Hancock	Robert Harrison	George Clinton	John Rutledge	John Milton	James Armstrong	Edward Telfair	Benjamin Lincoln
New Hampshire	5	5										
Massachusetts	10	10										
Connecticut	7	5	2									
New Jersey	6	1		5								
Pennsylvania	10	8			2							
Delaware	3			3								
Maryland	6					6						
Virginia	10	5		1	1		3					
South Carolina	7				1			6				
Georgia	5								2	1	1	1
Total	69	34	2	9	4	6	3	6	2	1	1	1

Voting for President

On February 4, 1789, 69 electors cast their votes. Each elector voted once for president and once for vice president. This chart shows who the electors voted for by state. Who was the next most popular leader after George Washington? Why do you think Washington received a vote from every elector in the electoral college?

new constitution. Delegates divided the federal government's power into three branches: executive, legislative, and judicial. They established a method of electing the president. The president would not be chosen directly by citizens. Each state would choose electors to cast votes for the president. This body of representatives is called the electoral college.

The first election took place on January 7, 1789. The 69 electors all chose one man they respected to lead the country. They elected George Washington.

PERSPECTIVES
Robert Yates

New York delegate Robert Yates spoke against the new Constitution. He felt it was flawed. Yates felt a strong central government would never represent the people. He said the country was too large. The people lived too far apart. Unhappy with the Constitution, Yates left the convention early. But he continued to argue his case in newspapers.

Washington's Inaugural Address

On April 16, 1789, Washington left Mount Vernon. People gathered along the 242-mile (389-km) route to wish him well. Eight days later, he arrived in the nation's capital, New York, to take the oath of office. Federal Hall was chaotic.

Newspapers reported there were so many people it might be possible to walk across their heads.

After taking the oath of office on April 30, 1789, Washington returned to the Senate chamber to address Congress. The new president's hands trembled as he pulled out a copy of his inaugural address. In it he spoke of his love for his country. He talked about the importance of national unity. Washington hoped the great experiment that was the new government of the United States would soon be respected around the world.

FURTHER EVIDENCE

Chapter One introduces George Washington. Identify one of the chapter's main points. What evidence does the author provide to support this point? The website at the link below discusses how Washington became president. How does the information on the website support what you read in this chapter? What new information does it provide?

Washington Becomes President
mycorelibrary.com/george-washington

CHAPTER TWO

UNEXPLORED GROUND

After his inauguration, Washington took charge of shaping his new role as leader of the United States. There was no model for him to follow. Every action he took set an example for future leaders. He wanted his actions to be based on strong principles. Mostly, he wanted to define clearly what it meant to be the leader of the United States.

Washington made many decisions concerning the role of the president. The US Constitution only provided a basic outline of the position.

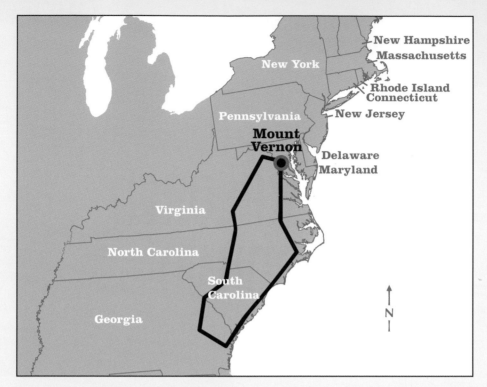

Southern Tour
In 1789 Washington toured New England. From April to June 1791, Washington visited the southern states. This map shows where he traveled on his southern tour. Why do you think Washington devoted so much time to traveling the nation?

On May 12, 1789, Washington wrote to his friend James Madison. He wondered how often a leader should meet with the public. He asked if private meetings with friends would be considered official visits. He spoke of touring the nation. Washington wanted everyone to have the chance to meet him.

At the same time Washington was thinking about his role, Congress was deciding what to call him. Congressman John Adams suggested Washington be known as His Highness the President of the United States. But most senators thought the name sounded too much like British royalty. Congress settled on the simpler title of President of the United States.

Running the Government

One of the president's duties is to appoint people to jobs in the federal government. In 1789, Congress created the Department of State, the Department of the Treasury, the Department of War, and the Office of the Attorney General. Washington spent much of 1789 filling nearly 1,000 new government positions.

Washington's friend Henry Knox became secretary of war. Lawyer Alexander Hamilton became secretary of the treasury. A former governor of Virginia, Edmund Randolph, became attorney general. Washington appointed fellow Virginian Thomas Jefferson as secretary of state.

From left: Washington, Knox, Hamilton, Jefferson, and Randolph

The First Advisors

The group of department heads became known as the president's cabinet. Washington valued their opinions. He tried to have a similarly close relationship with Congress. In August 1789, he appeared before the Senate. He wanted approval on a treaty with the Creek, a Native American nation. He believed the Constitution required him to appear in person.

Senators wanted more time to review the documents. They suggested that the issue go to a committee to be discussed further. This irritated Washington. He walked out and promised never to return. From then on, Washington sent the Senate all treaties in writing for approval.

Washington and the Court System

Washington wanted to have laws for the entire country. He thought they were needed to create a stronger union. But many Americans felt national laws might threaten their rights. In 1789 Washington and Congress began working on the judiciary branch of government.

On September 24, 1789, Washington signed the Judiciary Act into law. It established the federal court system. It outlined the powers granted to the courts. It created the Office of the Attorney General. Washington chose John Jay as chief justice of the Supreme Court. Jay firmly believed in a powerful national government.

Bill of Rights

Shortly after setting up federal courts, Congress began debating a bill of rights. Madison, a leading member of Congress, felt a bill of rights was needed. He felt Americans should have their rights protected in the Constitution. Lawmakers talked about the bill for months. Washington wrote to Congress in support of the new laws. In September 1789, Congress approved 12 constitutional amendments. Ten were adopted by the states. The Bill of Rights ensured freedom of speech, religion, and assembly, among other rights.

Washington received piles of letters from job seekers. In one case, a widow, Mary Wooster, wrote to Washington in search of a government job. In a letter to Wooster, written on May 21, 1789, Washington explained his situation:

I have duly received your affecting letter, dated the 8th day of this month. Sympathizing with you as I do in the great misfortunes, which have befallen your family in consequence of the war, my feelings as an individual would forcibly prompt me to do every thing in my power to repair those misfortunes. But as a public man, acting only with a reference to the public good, I must be allowed to decide upon all points of my duty, without consulting my private inclinations and wishes. I must be permitted, with the best lights I can obtain, and upon a general view of characters and circumstances, to nominate such persons alone to offices, as in my judgment shall be the best qualified to discharge the functions of the departments to which they shall be appointed.

Source: George Washington. "The Writings of George Washington, Vol. XI." Online Library of Liberty. Liberty Fund, Inc., August 14, 2015. Accessed June 21, 2015.

Point of View

Closely read this passage. What reasons does Washington give for not letting his feelings get in the way of his work? Do you agree with his position? Why or why not?

THE NATION'S ECONOMY

On January 8, 1790, Washington gave his first annual message to Congress. It came to be known as the State of the Union. In his address, Washington encouraged farming. He also spoke about the importance of manufacturing. He wanted a better system of roads and a larger postal service to connect the country. Washington's plans all required money.

The Revolutionary War freed the United States from British rule. The war also put the United States in debt.

Secretary of the Treasury Alexander Hamilton helped create the US financial system.

Fighting the British during the Revolutionary War had cost a lot of money. The federal government owed $40 million. To fund the war, it had borrowed money from Americans, as well as the French, Dutch, and Spanish governments. States also owed a total of more than $20 million to Americans. Lawmakers were unsure if the national government should pay off state debts. Washington firmly believed the United States should pay all debts.

Hamilton's Plan

Washington asked Alexander Hamilton to take on the country's debt problem. Hamilton clearly saw what needed to be done. On January 14, 1790, he gave his report to Congress. He wanted the government to take on the states' war debts. The federal government had no money to pay off the debts. So it would sell treasury bonds to the people. This would give the government money to use. Meanwhile, investors would earn interest from the government. The government would introduce new taxes so it could afford to pay interest to investors.

During the Revolutionary War, the government had offered a similar program. They gave soldiers and merchants certificates, promising to pay them later. But at the time, the government could not collect taxes. It could not raise money to pay people for their certificates. Many people sold their certificates. Some earned only pennies on the dollar.

Opposition to Hamilton's Plan

Hamilton's plan angered Madison. He called it unfair to the original certificate holders. With the new plan, they would never be fully paid for their services.

The government's plan to take on state war debts stirred up even more debate. People in the southern states did not feel they should help pay back the other states' debts. Some southern states, such as Virginia, had already paid down their debt. Washington believed Hamilton's plans were necessary to help the economy recover. But the split between northern and southern states worried him.

In July 1790, Congress agreed to the deal. In exchange, Washington's government supported building a new capital by the Potomac River. Virginians, such as Jefferson and Madison, thought the new capital might bring more trade and influence to the South.

National Bank

On December 15, 1790, Hamilton introduced the next step in the government's financial plan. He wanted to set up a national bank. The bank would be owned by the government and the public. It would establish a national currency. It would be a safe place for people

Hamilton, standing, needed to convince Washington and the cabinet his plan would successfully take care of the nation's debt.

to leave their money. And it would lend money to people. On January 20, 1791, the Senate approved the bank.

In the House of Representatives, Madison spoke against the bill, but it passed easily. On February 16, 1791, Washington asked Hamilton to defend his ideas. Hamilton wrote a 15,000-word reply. He said the Constitution gave some implied powers to the federal government. Hamilton's argument convinced

Washington. On February 25, Washington signed the National Bank Act.

Washington's support of Hamilton's plan split his cabinet. Jefferson was unhappy with Hamilton's influence on the president. Jefferson and Hamilton's differences led to the first political parties. Supporters of Hamilton were known as Federalists. Supporters of Jefferson were known as Republicans. They were later called Democratic-Republicans.

The split saddened Washington. He wanted to retire at the end of his first term. But Jefferson warned that without Washington, the North and the South might not stay together. Washington could not stand to see the country fall apart. In 1792 he ran for a second term. Once again, Washington received every electoral vote.

EXPLORE ONLINE

Chapter Three discusses opposition to the national bank. The website below talks about the difficulties in establishing the bank. As you know, every source is different. How is the information on this website different from the information you read in this chapter? How is it the same? How does reading about the federal government's plans to establish a bank help you to understand the US economy?

Alexander Hamilton
mycorelibrary.com/george-washington

CHAPTER FOUR

HOME AND ABROAD

Washington faced several challenges during his second term as president. The first came from 3,000 miles (4,828 km) away in France. Weeks after Washington took his second oath of office in 1793, the French Revolution (1787–1799) turned more violent. Mobs killed the French king. Soon a war broke out between France and Britain.

During the French Revolution, French citizens overthrew the monarchy.

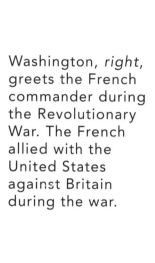

Washington, *right*, greets the French commander during the Revolutionary War. The French allied with the United States against Britain during the war.

Washington feared the United States could become caught up in the war. He knew the war was a threat to the US economy. Britain was the United States' largest trading partner. Washington met with his cabinet to plan. On April 22, 1793, Washington declared the United States neutral. This meant the country was not on either side of the war.

Some Americans accused the president of siding with Britain. Many people wanted the United States to support France. French troops had helped Americans fight for independence from Britain. But Washington planned to keep the United States "friendly and impartial" in the war. Members of Washington's cabinet were not neutral. Jefferson and the Republicans supported France. Hamilton and the Federalists stood firmly with Britain.

The New French Minister

After Washington's announcement, France's new ambassador to the United States arrived. His name was Edmond Genêt. Crowds of French

Causing Trouble

Edmond Genêt was sent to North America to gain US support for France's war with Britain. When Genêt arrived, he started hiring US sailors. He wanted to use their ships to pester the British fleet. He tried to turn US ports into French military bases. He claimed the 1778 alliance between France and the United States allowed him to do such things. Genêt also planned a takeover of Spanish-held Louisiana.

The British navy captured American sailors and forced them to work on British ships. This practice was called impressment.

supporters greeted him. He openly pushed for US support for the French cause.

Hamilton and Senator Rufus King urged Washington to take action. In August 1793, all members of Washington's cabinet agreed that Genêt's actions were wrong. Washington asked France to take back its ambassador. But power had again shifted in France. The new French government did not trust Genêt. It seemed his life would be in danger if he went back to France. Washington allowed him to stay in the United States.

British Aggression

Meanwhile, Britain tested US neutrality. By December 1793, they had seized 250 US ships suspected of carrying French goods.

The British forced US sailors to serve in the British navy. In addition, the British armed Native Americans against US settlers near the Great Lakes. Washington had to act before the situation got out of hand. He took action in the spring of 1794.

PERSPECTIVES
Native American Resistance

The British openly sold weapons to multiple Native American nations near the Great Lakes. The nations grouped together to protect their lands from settlers. The group was called the Western Confederacy. Starting in 1790, conflicts between the Confederacy and settlers became more common. In 1794 Washington sent Major General Anthony Wayne to take control of the area. The Native Americans asked the British for help. The British turned them down. The Confederacy surrendered.

Washington sent Chief Justice John Jay to London, England. Jay was to settle the disputes between the two countries.

Unease at Home

In July 1794, Washington's government faced another crisis. Some farmers rebelled over a 1791 federal tax on alcohol. The tax began as a way to pay down war debt. Over the years, anger grew. Rebels in western Pennsylvania attacked tax inspectors. In the summer of 1794, the rebels burned down one inspector's home.

Washington could not allow people to ignore the law. On August 2, 1794, he met with his cabinet. Hamilton and Knox suggested using military force against the rebels. Washington did not want to take such strong action. He hoped people would come to their senses. On August 7, Washington warned the rebels. They had until September 1 to obey the laws. Washington left nothing to chance. He readied 13,000 men to fight.

Washington led troops into Pennsylvania to stop a violent rebellion in 1794. The uprising started because of taxes on transporting alcohol.

By September, talks had failed. On September 19, 1794, Washington led troops to Pennsylvania. The rebels fled. Washington's actions showed that the government could collect taxes and enforce laws. But Jefferson and Madison found the show of force troubling.

Jay's Treaty

Washington's representative in Britain, Chief Justice John Jay, reached an agreement with Britain in the fall of 1794. News of Jay's Treaty traveled slowly back to

Many Americans were unhappy about the treaty US diplomat John Jay signed with Britain on November 19, 1794.

the United States. Washington learned the details on March 7, 1795. The deal was not what he had hoped for. The treaty failed to protect US trade. And the British still had troops by the Canadian border.

Americans were upset. They spoke out against Washington. Washington felt it was better to have a trade deal than none at all. Most importantly, the treaty helped avoid war with Britain.

On June 8, 1795, Washington sent the deal to Congress for approval. The treaty passed on June 24 by a vote of 20 to 10. Angry Americans took to the streets. Mobs surrounded the President's House in Philadelphia to protest the treaty.

Leaving Office

After Washington backed Jay's Treaty, the public did not fully support him. The split between Federalists and Republicans grew. Debates over Washington's decisions and personal attacks on his character strongly affected him.

On September 17, 1796, Washington announced he would retire at the end of his second term. He asked Americans to begin thinking about "common national interests."

On March 4, 1797, power smoothly passed from George Washington to the newly elected John Adams. The country Washington had once called "the last great experiment" was a success. On

Congress organized a funeral procession for Washington. The ceremony took place in Philadelphia, the nation's capital at the time, on December 26, 1799.

December 14, 1799, Washington died. Americans were very sad over the loss of such a great leader.

During Washington's career, he put the country's needs before his own. He set many good examples for future leaders. He kept the young country out of war when Britain and France ignored his wishes. More than 200 years later, Washington is still known as the "Father of his Country." The United States capital, as well as many monuments and buildings, are named in honor of the first president.

When George Washington became president, the press spoke of him in glowing terms. But this changed by the end of his first term. The Miller Center, a presidential research center, discusses Washington's reaction to criticism over Jay's Treaty:

> A final precedent set by America's first President, while unpleasant for Washington, was beneficial to his nation. Newspapers sympathetic to the Jeffersonians, emboldened by the public controversy surrounding the treaty with England, became increasingly critical of Washington during his final two years in office. One called him "Saint Washington," another mockingly offered him a crown. To the President's considerable credit, he bore these attacks with dignity—not even responding to them publicly.
>
> Source: "George Washington: Foreign Affairs." Miller Center of Public Affairs. University of Virginia, n.d. Web. Accessed July 9, 2015.

Changing Minds

Imagine you are one of George Washington's supporters. How would you defend him from these attacks? Make sure to explain your opinion. Include facts and details to support your opinion.

IMPORTANT DATES

1775

George Washington becomes leader of the Continental Army.

1783

Washington resigns as leader of the Continental Army on December 23.

1787

Washington leads the Constitutional Convention in Philadelphia.

1792

The electoral college elects Washington to a second term.

1794

Washington uses force to put down an uprising over federal taxes on September 19.

1795

The United States and Britain sign Jay's Treaty on June 24.

1789

Washington becomes the first president of the United States on April 30.

1790

Washington selects a site by the Potomac River for the nation's capital.

1791

Washington establishes a national bank on February 25.

1796

On September 17, Washington announces he will not seek a third term.

1797

Washington retires to Mount Vernon.

1799

Washington dies on December 14.

STOP AND THINK

Another View

This book explains how George Washington decided not to take sides in the French Revolution. As you know, every source is different. Ask an adult, such as a librarian, to help you find another source about this event. Write a short essay comparing and contrasting the new source's point of view with that of this book's author. How are they similar and why? How are they different and why?

Tell the Tale

Chapter One of this book discusses the excitement surrounding George Washington's first inauguration. Imagine you are making your way to see him at Federal Hall in New York City. Write 200 words about the people you encounter and the sights and sounds you experience. Are people happy or reluctant about the idea of having a president?

Surprise Me

Chapter Three discusses the conflict between two of Washington's cabinet secretaries, Thomas Jefferson and Alexander Hamilton. After reading this book, what two or three facts about their conflict did you find most surprising? Write a few sentences about each fact. Why did you find each fact surprising?

Why Do I Care?

George Washington believed in a strong central government. How might the United States be different if individual states still held more power than the central government? How might this change your life?

GLOSSARY

amendment
a change to a country's constitution

cabinet
a group of advisers to the president

constitution
the belief and law of a nation

economy
the system a country uses to manage its resources and money

inauguration
a ceremony held at the beginning of a president's term in office

interest
a charge for borrowing money

legislative branch
the branch of government that makes laws

militia
a military force of civilians

neutral
not taking sides in a fight

treasury bond
an investment in which an investor loans the government money and receives interest in return

treaty
a formal agreement between countries

LEARN MORE

Books

Calkhoven, Laurie. *George Washington: An American Life*. New York: Sterling Publishing Company, 2007.

Hamilton, John. *Turning Points of the American Revolution*. Minneapolis, MN: Abdo Publishing, 2013.

Websites

To learn more about Presidential Perspectives, visit **booklinks.abdopublishing.com**. These links are routinely monitored and updated to provide the most current information available.

Visit **mycorelibrary.com** for free additional tools for teachers and students.

INDEX

ABOUT THE AUTHOR

Anita Yasuda is the author of more than 100 books for children. She lives with her family in Huntington Beach, California, where you can find her on most days walking her dog along the shore.